2 0 2 1

This Planner

BELONGS TO

_____

_____

_____

Daily Appointment
P L A N N E R

· · · · · · · · · · · · · · · ·

2021/2022 CALENDAR OVERVIEW

DATED APPOINTMENT SCHEDULING

15 MIN INCREMENTS - 52 WEEKS

NOTES

CLIENT CONTACT DETAILS

PASSWORD TRACKER

2021

January

S	M	T	W	T	F	S
					1	2
3	4	5	6	7	8	9
10	11	12	13	14	15	16
17	18	19	20	21	22	23
24	25	26	27	28	29	30
31						

February

S	M	T	W	T	F	S
	1	2	3	4	5	6
7	8	9	10	11	12	13
14	15	16	17	18	19	20
21	22	23	24	25	26	27
28						

March

S	M	T	W	T	F	S
	1	2	3	4	5	6
7	8	9	10	11	12	13
14	15	16	17	18	19	20
21	22	23	24	25	26	27
28	29	30	31			

April

S	M	T	W	T	F	S
				1	2	3
4	5	6	7	8	9	10
11	12	13	14	15	16	17
18	19	20	21	22	23	24
25	26	27	28	29	30	

May

S	M	T	W	T	F	S
						1
2	3	4	5	6	7	8
9	10	11	12	13	14	15
16	17	18	19	20	21	22
23	24	25	26	27	28	29
30	31					

June

S	M	T	W	T	F	S
		1	2	3	4	5
6	7	8	9	10	11	12
13	14	15	16	17	18	19
20	21	22	23	24	25	26
27	28	29	30			

July

S	M	T	W	T	F	S
				1	2	3
4	5	6	7	8	9	10
11	12	13	14	15	16	17
18	19	20	21	22	23	24
25	26	27	28	29	30	31

August

S	M	T	W	T	F	S
1	2	3	4	5	6	7
8	9	10	11	12	13	14
15	16	17	18	19	20	21
22	23	24	25	26	27	28
29	30	31				

September

S	M	T	W	T	F	S
			1	2	3	4
5	6	7	8	9	10	11
12	13	14	15	16	17	18
19	20	21	22	23	24	25
26	27	28	29	30		

October

S	M	T	W	T	F	S
					1	2
3	4	5	6	7	8	9
10	11	12	13	14	15	16
17	18	19	20	21	22	23
24	25	26	27	28	29	30
31						

November

S	M	T	W	T	F	S
	1	2	3	4	5	6
7	8	9	10	11	12	13
14	15	16	17	18	19	20
21	22	23	24	25	26	27
28	29	30				

December

S	M	T	W	T	F	S
		1	2	3	4	
5	6	7	8	9	10	11
12	13	14	15	16	17	18
19	20	21	22	23	24	25
26	27	28	29	30	31	

2022

January

S	M	T	W	T	F	S
						1
2	3	4	5	6	7	8
9	10	11	12	13	14	15
16	17	18	19	20	21	22
23	24	25	26	27	28	29
30	31					

February

S	M	T	W	T	F	S
		1	2	3	4	5
6	7	8	9	10	11	12
13	14	15	16	17	18	19
20	21	22	23	24	25	26
27	28					

March

S	M	T	W	T	F	S
		1	2	3	4	5
6	7	8	9	10	11	12
13	14	15	16	17	18	19
20	21	22	23	24	25	26
27	28	29	30	31		

April

S	M	T	W	T	F	S
					1	2
3	4	5	6	7	8	9
10	11	12	13	14	15	16
17	18	19	20	21	22	23
24	25	26	27	28	29	30

May

S	M	T	W	T	F	S
1	2	3	4	5	6	7
8	9	10	11	12	13	14
15	16	17	18	19	20	21
22	23	24	25	26	27	28
29	30	31				

June

S	M	T	W	T	F	S
			1	2	3	4
5	6	7	8	9	10	11
12	13	14	15	16	17	18
19	20	21	22	23	24	25
26	27	28	29	30		

July

S	M	T	W	T	F	S
					1	2
3	4	5	6	7	8	9
10	11	12	13	14	15	16
17	18	19	20	21	22	23
24	25	26	27	28	29	30
31						

August

S	M	T	W	T	F	S
	1	2	3	4	5	6
7	8	9	10	11	12	13
14	15	16	17	18	19	20
21	22	23	24	25	26	27
28	29	30	31			

September

S	M	T	W	T	F	S
				1	2	3
4	5	6	7	8	9	10
11	12	13	14	15	16	17
18	19	20	21	22	23	24
25	26	27	28	29	30	

October

S	M	T	W	T	F	S
						1
2	3	4	5	6	7	8
9	10	11	12	13	14	15
16	17	18	19	20	21	22
23	24	25	26	27	28	29
30	31					

November

S	M	T	W	T	F	S
		1	2	3	4	5
6	7	8	9	10	11	12
13	14	15	16	17	18	19
20	21	22	23	24	25	26
27	28	29	30			

December

S	M	T	W	T	F	S
				1	2	3
4	5	6	7	8	9	10
11	12	13	14	15	16	17
18	19	20	21	22	23	24
25	26	27	28	29	30	31

		Mon 28 December	Tue 29 December	Wed 30 December	Thu 31 December
6 am	00 15 30 45				
7 am	00 15 30 45				
8 am	00 15 30 45				
9 am	00 15 30 45				
10 am	00 15 30 45				
11 am	00 15 30 45				
12 pm	00 15 30 45				
1 pm	00 15 30 45				
2 pm	00 15 30 45				
3 pm	00 15 30 45				
4 pm	00 15 30 45				
5 pm	00 15 30 45				
6 pm	00 15 30 45				
7 pm	00 15 30 45				
8 pm	00 15 30 45				
9 pm	00 15 30 45				
10 pm	00 15 30 45				

		Fri	1 January	Sat	2 January	Sun	3 January	Notes
6 am	00 / 15 / 30 / 45							
7 am	00 / 15 / 30 / 45							
8 am	00 / 15 / 30 / 45							
9 am	00 / 15 / 30 / 45							
10 am	00 / 15 / 30 / 45							
11 am	00 / 15 / 30 / 45							
12 pm	00 / 15 / 30 / 45							
1 pm	00 / 15 / 30 / 45							
2 pm	00 / 15 / 30 / 45							
3 pm	00 / 15 / 30 / 45							
4 pm	00 / 15 / 30 / 45							
5 pm	00 / 15 / 30 / 45							
6 pm	00 / 15 / 30 / 45							
7 pm	00 / 15 / 30 / 45							
8 pm	00 / 15 / 30 / 45							
9 pm	00 / 15 / 30 / 45							
10 pm	00 / 15 / 30 / 45	Fri		Sat		Sun		

		Mon 4 January	Tue 5 January	Wed 6 January	Thu 7 January
6 am	00 15 30 45				
7 am	00 15 30 45				
8 am	00 15 30 45				
9 am	00 15 30 45				
10 am	00 15 30 45				
11 am	00 15 30 45				
12 pm	00 15 30 45				
1 pm	00 15 30 45				
2 pm	00 15 30 45				
3 pm	00 15 30 45				
4 pm	00 15 30 45				
5 pm	00 15 30 45				
6 pm	00 15 30 45				
7 pm	00 15 30 45				
8 pm	00 15 30 45				
9 pm	00 15 30 45				
10 pm	00 15 30 45				

		Fri	8 January	Sat	9 January	Sun	10 January	Notes
6 am	00 15 30 45							
7 am	00 15 30 45							
8 am	00 15 30 45							
9 am	00 15 30 45							
10 am	00 15 30 45							
11 am	00 15 30 45							
12 pm	00 15 30 45							
1 pm	00 15 30 45							
2 pm	00 15 30 45							
3 pm	00 15 30 45							
4 pm	00 15 30 45							
5 pm	00 15 30 45							
6 pm	00 15 30 45							
7 pm	00 15 30 45							
8 pm	00 15 30 45							
9 pm	00 15 30 45							
10 pm	00 15 30 45							

		Mon 11 January	Tue 12 January	Wed 13 January	Thu 14 January
6 am	00 15 30 45				
7 am	00 15 30 45				
8 am	00 15 30 45				
9 am	00 15 30 45				
10 am	00 15 30 45				
11 am	00 15 30 45				
12 pm	00 15 30 45				
1 pm	00 15 30 45				
2 pm	00 15 30 45				
3 pm	00 15 30 45				
4 pm	00 15 30 45				
5 pm	00 15 30 45				
6 pm	00 15 30 45				
7 pm	00 15 30 45				
8 pm	00 15 30 45				
9 pm	00 15 30 45				
10 pm	00 15 30 45				

		Fri 15 January	Sat 16 January	Sun 17 January	Notes
6 am	00 15 30 45				
7 am	00 15 30 45				
8 am	00 15 30 45				
9 am	00 15 30 45				
10 am	00 15 30 45				
11 am	00 15 30 45				
12 pm	00 15 30 45				
1 pm	00 15 30 45				
2 pm	00 15 30 45				
3 pm	00 15 30 45				
4 pm	00 15 30 45				
5 pm	00 15 30 45				
6 pm	00 15 30 45				
7 pm	00 15 30 45				
8 pm	00 15 30 45				
9 pm	00 15 30 45				
10 pm	00 15 30 45				

	Mon 18 January	Tue 19 January	Wed 20 January	Thu 21 January
6 am				
7 am				
8 am				
9 am				
10 am				
11 am				
12 pm				
1 pm				
2 pm				
3 pm				
4 pm				
5 pm				
6 pm				
7 pm				
8 pm				
9 pm				
10 pm				

	Fri 22 January	Sat 23 January	Sun 24 January	Notes
6 am				
7 am				
8 am				
9 am				
10 am				
11 am				
12 pm				
1 pm				
2 pm				
3 pm				
4 pm				
5 pm				
6 pm				
7 pm				
8 pm				
9 pm				
10 pm				

		Mon 25 January	Tue 26 January	Wed 27 January	Thu 28 January
6 am	00 15 30 45				
7 am	00 15 30 45				
8 am	00 15 30 45				
9 am	00 15 30 45				
10 am	00 15 30 45				
11 am	00 15 30 45				
12 pm	00 15 30 45				
1 pm	00 15 30 45				
2 pm	00 15 30 45				
3 pm	00 15 30 45				
4 pm	00 15 30 45				
5 pm	00 15 30 45				
6 pm	00 15 30 45				
7 pm	00 15 30 45				
8 pm	00 15 30 45				
9 pm	00 15 30 45				
10 pm	00 15 30 45				

		Fri	29 January	Sat	30 January	Sun	31 January	Notes
6 am	00 15 30 45							
7 am	00 15 30 45							
8 am	00 15 30 45							
9 am	00 15 30 45							
10 am	00 15 30 45							
11 am	00 15 30 45							
12 pm	00 15 30 45							
1 pm	00 15 30 45							
2 pm	00 15 30 45							
3 pm	00 15 30 45							
4 pm	00 15 30 45							
5 pm	00 15 30 45							
6 pm	00 15 30 45							
7 pm	00 15 30 45							
8 pm	00 15 30 45							
9 pm	00 15 30 45							
10 pm	00 15 30 45							

		Mon 1 February	Tue 2 February	Wed 3 February	Thu 4 February
6 am	00 15 30 45				
7 am	00 15 30 45				
8 am	00 15 30 45				
9 am	00 15 30 45				
10 am	00 15 30 45				
11 am	00 15 30 45				
12 pm	00 15 30 45				
1 pm	00 15 30 45				
2 pm	00 15 30 45				
3 pm	00 15 30 45				
4 pm	00 15 30 45				
5 pm	00 15 30 45				
6 pm	00 15 30 45				
7 pm	00 15 30 45				
8 pm	00 15 30 45				
9 pm	00 15 30 45				
10 pm	00 15 30 45				

		Fri 5 February	Sat 6 February	Sun 7 February	Notes
6 am	00 15 30 45				
7 am	00 15 30 45				
8 am	00 15 30 45				
9 am	00 15 30 45				
10 am	00 15 30 45				
11 am	00 15 30 45				
12 pm	00 15 30 45				
1 pm	00 15 30 45				
2 pm	00 15 30 45				
3 pm	00 15 30 45				
4 pm	00 15 30 45				
5 pm	00 15 30 45				
6 pm	00 15 30 45				
7 pm	00 15 30 45				
8 pm	00 15 30 45				
9 pm	00 15 30 45				
10 pm	00 15 30 45				

		Mon 8 February	Tue 9 February	Wed 10 February	Thu 11 February
6 am	00 15 30 45				
7 am	00 15 30 45				
8 am	00 15 30 45				
9 am	00 15 30 45				
10 am	00 15 30 45				
11 am	00 15 30 45				
12 pm	00 15 30 45				
1 pm	00 15 30 45				
2 pm	00 15 30 45				
3 pm	00 15 30 45				
4 pm	00 15 30 45				
5 pm	00 15 30 45				
6 pm	00 15 30 45				
7 pm	00 15 30 45				
8 pm	00 15 30 45				
9 pm	00 15 30 45				
10 pm	00 15 30 45				

		Fri 12 February	Sat 13 February	Sun 14 February	Notes
6 am	00 15 30 45				
7 am	00 15 30 45				
8 am	00 15 30 45				
9 am	00 15 30 45				
10 am	00 15 30 45				
11 am	00 15 30 45				
12 pm	00 15 30 45				
1 pm	00 15 30 45				
2 pm	00 15 30 45				
3 pm	00 15 30 45				
4 pm	00 15 30 45				
5 pm	00 15 30 45				
6 pm	00 15 30 45				
7 pm	00 15 30 45				
8 pm	00 15 30 45				
9 pm	00 15 30 45				
10 pm	00 15 30 45				

		Mon 15 February	Tue 16 February	Wed 17 February	Thu 18 February
6 am	00 15 30 45				
7 am	00 15 30 45				
8 am	00 15 30 45				
9 am	00 15 30 45				
10 am	00 15 30 45				
11 am	00 15 30 45				
12 pm	00 15 30 45				
1 pm	00 15 30 45				
2 pm	00 15 30 45				
3 pm	00 15 30 45				
4 pm	00 15 30 45				
5 pm	00 15 30 45				
6 pm	00 15 30 45				
7 pm	00 15 30 45				
8 pm	00 15 30 45				
9 pm	00 15 30 45				
10 pm	00 15 30 45				

		Fri 19 February	Sat 20 February	Sun 21 February	Notes
6 am	00 15 30 45				
7 am	00 15 30 45				
8 am	00 15 30 45				
9 am	00 15 30 45				
10 am	00 15 30 45				
11 am	00 15 30 45				
12 pm	00 15 30 45				
1 pm	00 15 30 45				
2 pm	00 15 30 45				
3 pm	00 15 30 45				
4 pm	00 15 30 45				
5 pm	00 15 30 45				
6 pm	00 15 30 45				
7 pm	00 15 30 45				
8 pm	00 15 30 45				
9 pm	00 15 30 45				
10 pm	00 15 30 45				

		Mon 22 February	Tue 23 February	Wed 24 February	Thu 25 February
6 am	00 15 30 45				
7 am	00 15 30 45				
8 am	00 15 30 45				
9 am	00 15 30 45				
10 am	00 15 30 45				
11 am	00 15 30 45				
12 pm	00 15 30 45				
1 pm	00 15 30 45				
2 pm	00 15 30 45				
3 pm	00 15 30 45				
4 pm	00 15 30 45				
5 pm	00 15 30 45				
6 pm	00 15 30 45				
7 pm	00 15 30 45				
8 pm	00 15 30 45				
9 pm	00 15 30 45				
10 pm	00 15 30 45				

	Fri 26 February	Sat 27 February	Sun 28 February	Notes
6 am				
7 am				
8 am				
9 am				
10 am				
11 am				
12 pm				
1 pm				
2 pm				
3 pm				
4 pm				
5 pm				
6 pm				
7 pm				
8 pm				
9 pm				
10 pm				

	Mon 1 March	Tue 2 March	Wed 3 March	Thu 4 March
6 am				
7 am				
8 am				
9 am				
10 am				
11 am				
12 pm				
1 pm				
2 pm				
3 pm				
4 pm				
5 pm				
6 pm				
7 pm				
8 pm				
9 pm				
10 pm				

		Fri 5 March	Sat 6 March	Sun 7 March	Notes
6 am	00 / 15 / 30 / 45				
7 am	00 / 15 / 30 / 45				
8 am	00 / 15 / 30 / 45				
9 am	00 / 15 / 30 / 45				
10 am	00 / 15 / 30 / 45				
11 am	00 / 15 / 30 / 45				
12 pm	00 / 15 / 30 / 45				
1 pm	00 / 15 / 30 / 45				
2 pm	00 / 15 / 30 / 45				
3 pm	00 / 15 / 30 / 45				
4 pm	00 / 15 / 30 / 45				
5 pm	00 / 15 / 30 / 45				
6 pm	00 / 15 / 30 / 45				
7 pm	00 / 15 / 30 / 45				
8 pm	00 / 15 / 30 / 45				
9 pm	00 / 15 / 30 / 45				
10 pm	00 / 15 / 30 / 45				

		Mon 8 March	Tue 9 March	Wed 10 March	Thu 11 March
6 am	00 15 30 45				
7 am	00 15 30 45				
8 am	00 15 30 45				
9 am	00 15 30 45				
10 am	00 15 30 45				
11 am	00 15 30 45				
12 pm	00 15 30 45				
1 pm	00 15 30 45				
2 pm	00 15 30 45				
3 pm	00 15 30 45				
4 pm	00 15 30 45				
5 pm	00 15 30 45				
6 pm	00 15 30 45				
7 pm	00 15 30 45				
8 pm	00 15 30 45				
9 pm	00 15 30 45				
10 pm	00 15 30 45				

	Fri 12 March	Sat 13 March	Sun 14 March	Notes
6 am				
7 am				
8 am				
9 am				
10 am				
11 am				
12 pm				
1 pm				
2 pm				
3 pm				
4 pm				
5 pm				
6 pm				
7 pm				
8 pm				
9 pm				
10 pm				

	Mon 15 March	Tue 16 March	Wed 17 March	Thu 18 March
6 am				
7 am				
8 am				
9 am				
10 am				
11 am				
12 pm				
1 pm				
2 pm				
3 pm				
4 pm				
5 pm				
6 pm				
7 pm				
8 pm				
9 pm				
10 pm				

	Fri 19 March	Sat 20 March	Sun 21 March	Notes
6 am				
7 am				
8 am				
9 am				
10 am				
11 am				
12 pm				
1 pm				
2 pm				
3 pm				
4 pm				
5 pm				
6 pm				
7 pm				
8 pm				
9 pm				
10 pm				

		Mon 22 March	Tue 23 March	Wed 24 March	Thu 25 March
6 am	00 15 30 45				
7 am	00 15 30 45				
8 am	00 15 30 45				
9 am	00 15 30 45				
10 am	00 15 30 45				
11 am	00 15 30 45				
12 pm	00 15 30 45				
1 pm	00 15 30 45				
2 pm	00 15 30 45				
3 pm	00 15 30 45				
4 pm	00 15 30 45				
5 pm	00 15 30 45				
6 pm	00 15 30 45				
7 pm	00 15 30 45				
8 pm	00 15 30 45				
9 pm	00 15 30 45				
10 pm	00 15 30 45				

	Fri 26 March	Sat 27 March	Sun 28 March	Notes
6 am				
7 am				
8 am				
9 am				
10 am				
11 am				
12 pm				
1 pm				
2 pm				
3 pm				
4 pm				
5 pm				
6 pm				
7 pm				
8 pm				
9 pm				
10 pm				

	Mon 29 March	Tue 30 March	Wed 31 March	Thu 1 April
6 am				
7 am				
8 am				
9 am				
10 am				
11 am				
12 pm				
1 pm				
2 pm				
3 pm				
4 pm				
5 pm				
6 pm				
7 pm				
8 pm				
9 pm				
10 pm				

	Fri 2 April	Sat 3 April	Sun 4 April	Notes
6 am				
7 am				
8 am				
9 am				
10 am				
11 am				
12 pm				
1 pm				
2 pm				
3 pm				
4 pm				
5 pm				
6 pm				
7 pm				
8 pm				
9 pm				
10 pm	Fri 2 April	Sat 3 April	Sun 4 April	

		Mon	5 April	Tue	6 April	Wed	7 April	Thu	8 April
6 am	00 15 30 45								
7 am	00 15 30 45								
8 am	00 15 30 45								
9 am	00 15 30 45								
10 am	00 15 30 45								
11 am	00 15 30 45								
12 pm	00 15 30 45								
1 pm	00 15 30 45								
2 pm	00 15 30 45								
3 pm	00 15 30 45								
4 pm	00 15 30 45								
5 pm	00 15 30 45								
6 pm	00 15 30 45								
7 pm	00 15 30 45								
8 pm	00 15 30 45								
9 pm	00 15 30 45								
10 pm	00 15 30 45								

	Fri 9 April	Sat 10 April	Sun 11 April	Notes
6 am				
7 am				
8 am				
9 am				
10 am				
11 am				
12 pm				
1 pm				
2 pm				
3 pm				
4 pm				
5 pm				
6 pm				
7 pm				
8 pm				
9 pm				
10 pm				

	Mon 12 APRIL	Tue 13 APRIL	Wed 14 APRIL	Thu 15 APRIL
6 am				
7 am				
8 am				
9 am				
10 am				
11 am				
12 pm				
1 pm				
2 pm				
3 pm				
4 pm				
5 pm				
6 pm				
7 pm				
8 pm				
9 pm				
10 pm				

	Fri 16 April	Sat 17 April	Sun 18 April	Notes
6 am				
7 am				
8 am				
9 am				
10 am				
11 am				
12 pm				
1 pm				
2 pm				
3 pm				
4 pm				
5 pm				
6 pm				
7 pm				
8 pm				
9 pm				
10 pm				

		Mon 19 April	Tue 20 April	Wed 21 April	Thu 22 April
6 am	00 15 30 45				
7 am	00 15 30 45				
8 am	00 15 30 45				
9 am	00 15 30 45				
10 am	00 15 30 45				
11 am	00 15 30 45				
12 pm	00 15 30 45				
1 pm	00 15 30 45				
2 pm	00 15 30 45				
3 pm	00 15 30 45				
4 pm	00 15 30 45				
5 pm	00 15 30 45				
6 pm	00 15 30 45				
7 pm	00 15 30 45				
8 pm	00 15 30 45				
9 pm	00 15 30 45				
10 pm	00 15 30 45				

		Fri 23 April	Sat 24 April	Sun 25 April	Notes
6 am	00 15 30 45				
7 am	00 15 30 45				
8 am	00 15 30 45				
9 am	00 15 30 45				
10 am	00 15 30 45				
11 am	00 15 30 45				
12 pm	00 15 30 45				
1 pm	00 15 30 45				
2 pm	00 15 30 45				
3 pm	00 15 30 45				
4 pm	00 15 30 45				
5 pm	00 15 30 45				
6 pm	00 15 30 45				
7 pm	00 15 30 45				
8 pm	00 15 30 45				
9 pm	00 15 30 45				
10 pm	00 15 30 45				

	Mon 26 April	Tue 27 April	Wed 28 April	Thu 29 April
6 am				
7 am				
8 am				
9 am				
10 am				
11 am				
12 pm				
1 pm				
2 pm				
3 pm				
4 pm				
5 pm				
6 pm				
7 pm				
8 pm				
9 pm				
10 pm				

		Fri	30 April	Sat	1 May	Sun	2 May	Notes
6 am	00 15 30 45							
7 am	00 15 30 45							
8 am	00 15 30 45							
9 am	00 15 30 45							
10 am	00 15 30 45							
11 am	00 15 30 45							
12 pm	00 15 30 45							
1 pm	00 15 30 45							
2 pm	00 15 30 45							
3 pm	00 15 30 45							
4 pm	00 15 30 45							
5 pm	00 15 30 45							
6 pm	00 15 30 45							
7 pm	00 15 30 45							
8 pm	00 15 30 45							
9 pm	00 15 30 45							
10 pm	00 15 30 45	Fri	30 April	Sat	1 May	Sun	2 May	

		Mon 3 May	Tue 4 May	Wed 5 May	Thu 6 May
6 am	00 15 30 45				
7 am	00 15 30 45				
8 am	00 15 30 45				
9 am	00 15 30 45				
10 am	00 15 30 45				
11 am	00 15 30 45				
12 pm	00 15 30 45				
1 pm	00 15 30 45				
2 pm	00 15 30 45				
3 pm	00 15 30 45				
4 pm	00 15 30 45				
5 pm	00 15 30 45				
6 pm	00 15 30 45				
7 pm	00 15 30 45				
8 pm	00 15 30 45				
9 pm	00 15 30 45				
10 pm	00 15 30 45				

		Fri 7 May	Sat 8 May	Sun 9 May	Notes
6 am	00 15 30 45				
7 am	00 15 30 45				
8 am	00 15 30 45				
9 am	00 15 30 45				
10 am	00 15 30 45				
11 am	00 15 30 45				
12 pm	00 15 30 45				
1 pm	00 15 30 45				
2 pm	00 15 30 45				
3 pm	00 15 30 45				
4 pm	00 15 30 45				
5 pm	00 15 30 45				
6 pm	00 15 30 45				
7 pm	00 15 30 45				
8 pm	00 15 30 45				
9 pm	00 15 30 45				
10 pm	00 15 30 45				

	Mon 10 May	Tue 11 May	Wed 12 May	Thu 13 May
6 am				
7 am				
8 am				
9 am				
10 am				
11 am				
12 pm				
1 pm				
2 pm				
3 pm				
4 pm				
5 pm				
6 pm				
7 pm				
8 pm				
9 pm				
10 pm				

	Fri 14 May	Sat 15 May	Sun 16 May	Notes
6 am				
7 am				
8 am				
9 am				
10 am				
11 am				
12 pm				
1 pm				
2 pm				
3 pm				
4 pm				
5 pm				
6 pm				
7 pm				
8 pm				
9 pm				
10 pm				

		Mon 17 May	Tue 18 May	Wed 19 May	Thu 20 May
6 am	00 15 30 45				
7 am	00 15 30 45				
8 am	00 15 30 45				
9 am	00 15 30 45				
10 am	00 15 30 45				
11 am	00 15 30 45				
12 pm	00 15 30 45				
1 pm	00 15 30 45				
2 pm	00 15 30 45				
3 pm	00 15 30 45				
4 pm	00 15 30 45				
5 pm	00 15 30 45				
6 pm	00 15 30 45				
7 pm	00 15 30 45				
8 pm	00 15 30 45				
9 pm	00 15 30 45				
10 pm	00 15 30 45				

		Fri 21 May	Sat 22 May	Sun 23 May	Notes
6 am	00 15 30 45				
7 am	00 15 30 45				
8 am	00 15 30 45				
9 am	00 15 30 45				
10 am	00 15 30 45				
11 am	00 15 30 45				
12 pm	00 15 30 45				
1 pm	00 15 30 45				
2 pm	00 15 30 45				
3 pm	00 15 30 45				
4 pm	00 15 30 45				
5 pm	00 15 30 45				
6 pm	00 15 30 45				
7 pm	00 15 30 45				
8 pm	00 15 30 45				
9 pm	00 15 30 45				
10 pm	00 15 30 45				

		Mon 24 May	Tue 25 May	Wed 26 May	Thu 27 May
6 am	00 15 30 45				
7 am	00 15 30 45				
8 am	00 15 30 45				
9 am	00 15 30 45				
10 am	00 15 30 45				
11 am	00 15 30 45				
12 pm	00 15 30 45				
1 pm	00 15 30 45				
2 pm	00 15 30 45				
3 pm	00 15 30 45				
4 pm	00 15 30 45				
5 pm	00 15 30 45				
6 pm	00 15 30 45				
7 pm	00 15 30 45				
8 pm	00 15 30 45				
9 pm	00 15 30 45				
10 pm	00 15 30 45				

	Fri 28 May	Sat 29 May	Sun 30 May	Notes
6 am				
7 am				
8 am				
9 am				
10 am				
11 am				
12 pm				
1 pm				
2 pm				
3 pm				
4 pm				
5 pm				
6 pm				
7 pm				
8 pm				
9 pm				
10 pm				

		Mon	31 May	Tue	1 June	Wed	2 June	Thu	3 June
6 am	00 15 30 45								
7 am	00 15 30 45								
8 am	00 15 30 45								
9 am	00 15 30 45								
10 am	00 15 30 45								
11 am	00 15 30 45								
12 pm	00 15 30 45								
1 pm	00 15 30 45								
2 pm	00 15 30 45								
3 pm	00 15 30 45								
4 pm	00 15 30 45								
5 pm	00 15 30 45								
6 pm	00 15 30 45								
7 pm	00 15 30 45								
8 pm	00 15 30 45								
9 pm	00 15 30 45								
10 pm	00 15 30 45								

		Fri	4 June	Sat	5 June	Sun	6 June	Notes
6 am	00 15 30 45							
7 am	00 15 30 45							
8 am	00 15 30 45							
9 am	00 15 30 45							
10 am	00 15 30 45							
11 am	00 15 30 45							
12 pm	00 15 30 45							
1 pm	00 15 30 45							
2 pm	00 15 30 45							
3 pm	00 15 30 45							
4 pm	00 15 30 45							
5 pm	00 15 30 45							
6 pm	00 15 30 45							
7 pm	00 15 30 45							
8 pm	00 15 30 45							
9 pm	00 15 30 45							
10 pm	00 15 30 45							

		Mon	7 June	Tue	8 June	Wed	9 June	Thu	10 June
6 am	00 15 30 45								
7 am	00 15 30 45								
8 am	00 15 30 45								
9 am	00 15 30 45								
10 am	00 15 30 45								
11 am	00 15 30 45								
12 pm	00 15 30 45								
1 pm	00 15 30 45								
2 pm	00 15 30 45								
3 pm	00 15 30 45								
4 pm	00 15 30 45								
5 pm	00 15 30 45								
6 pm	00 15 30 45								
7 pm	00 15 30 45								
8 pm	00 15 30 45								
9 pm	00 15 30 45								
10 pm	00 15 30 45								

		Fri 11 June	Sat 12 June	Sun 13 June	Notes
6 am	00 15 30 45				
7 am	00 15 30 45				
8 am	00 15 30 45				
9 am	00 15 30 45				
10 am	00 15 30 45				
11 am	00 15 30 45				
12 pm	00 15 30 45				
1 pm	00 15 30 45				
2 pm	00 15 30 45				
3 pm	00 15 30 45				
4 pm	00 15 30 45				
5 pm	00 15 30 45				
6 pm	00 15 30 45				
7 pm	00 15 30 45				
8 pm	00 15 30 45				
9 pm	00 15 30 45				
10 pm	00 15 30 45				

		Mon 14 June	Tue 15 June	Wed 16 June	Thu 17 June
6 am	00 15 30 45				
7 am	00 15 30 45				
8 am	00 15 30 45				
9 am	00 15 30 45				
10 am	00 15 30 45				
11 am	00 15 30 45				
12 pm	00 15 30 45				
1 pm	00 15 30 45				
2 pm	00 15 30 45				
3 pm	00 15 30 45				
4 pm	00 15 30 45				
5 pm	00 15 30 45				
6 pm	00 15 30 45				
7 pm	00 15 30 45				
8 pm	00 15 30 45				
9 pm	00 15 30 45				
10 pm	00 15 30 45				

	Fri 18 June	Sat 19 June	Sun 20 June	Notes
6 am				
7 am				
8 am				
9 am				
10 am				
11 am				
12 pm				
1 pm				
2 pm				
3 pm				
4 pm				
5 pm				
6 pm				
7 pm				
8 pm				
9 pm				
10 pm				

	Mon 21 June	Tue 22 June	Wed 23 June	Thu 24 June
6 am				
7 am				
8 am				
9 am				
10 am				
11 am				
12 pm				
1 pm				
2 pm				
3 pm				
4 pm				
5 pm				
6 pm				
7 pm				
8 pm				
9 pm				
10 pm				

	Fri 25 June	Sat 26 June	Sun 27 June	Notes
6 am				
7 am				
8 am				
9 am				
10 am				
11 am				
12 pm				
1 pm				
2 pm				
3 pm				
4 pm				
5 pm				
6 pm				
7 pm				
8 pm				
9 pm				
10 pm				

	Mon 28 June	Tue 29 June	Wed 30 June	Thu 1 July
6 am				
7 am				
8 am				
9 am				
10 am				
11 am				
12 pm				
1 pm				
2 pm				
3 pm				
4 pm				
5 pm				
6 pm				
7 pm				
8 pm				
9 pm				
10 pm				

	Fri 2 July	Sat 3 July	Sun 4 July	Notes
6 am				
7 am				
8 am				
9 am				
10 am				
11 am				
12 pm				
1 pm				
2 pm				
3 pm				
4 pm				
5 pm				
6 pm				
7 pm				
8 pm				
9 pm				
10 pm				

	Mon 5 July	Tue 6 July	Wed 7 July	Thu 8 July
6 am				
7 am				
8 am				
9 am				
10 am				
11 am				
12 pm				
1 pm				
2 pm				
3 pm				
4 pm				
5 pm				
6 pm				
7 pm				
8 pm				
9 pm				
10 pm				

		Fri 9 July	Sat 10 July	Sun 11 July	Notes
6 am	00 15 30 45				
7 am	00 15 30 45				
8 am	00 15 30 45				
9 am	00 15 30 45				
10 am	00 15 30 45				
11 am	00 15 30 45				
12 pm	00 15 30 45				
1 pm	00 15 30 45				
2 pm	00 15 30 45				
3 pm	00 15 30 45				
4 pm	00 15 30 45				
5 pm	00 15 30 45				
6 pm	00 15 30 45				
7 pm	00 15 30 45				
8 pm	00 15 30 45				
9 pm	00 15 30 45				
10 pm	00 15 30 45				

		Mon	12 July	Tue	13 July	Wed	14 July	Thu	15 July
6 am	00 15 30 45								
7 am	00 15 30 45								
8 am	00 15 30 45								
9 am	00 15 30 45								
10 am	00 15 30 45								
11 am	00 15 30 45								
12 pm	00 15 30 45								
1 pm	00 15 30 45								
2 pm	00 15 30 45								
3 pm	00 15 30 45								
4 pm	00 15 30 45								
5 pm	00 15 30 45								
6 pm	00 15 30 45								
7 pm	00 15 30 45								
8 pm	00 15 30 45								
9 pm	00 15 30 45								
10 pm	00 15 30 45								

		Fri 16 July	Sat 17 July	Sun 18 July	Notes
6 am	00 15 30 45				
7 am	00 15 30 45				
8 am	00 15 30 45				
9 am	00 15 30 45				
10 am	00 15 30 45				
11 am	00 15 30 45				
12 pm	00 15 30 45				
1 pm	00 15 30 45				
2 pm	00 15 30 45				
3 pm	00 15 30 45				
4 pm	00 15 30 45				
5 pm	00 15 30 45				
6 pm	00 15 30 45				
7 pm	00 15 30 45				
8 pm	00 15 30 45				
9 pm	00 15 30 45				
10 pm	00 15 30 45				

		Mon 19 July	Tue 20 July	Wed 21 July	Thu 22 July
6 am	00 15 30 45				
7 am	00 15 30 45				
8 am	00 15 30 45				
9 am	00 15 30 45				
10 am	00 15 30 45				
11 am	00 15 30 45				
12 pm	00 15 30 45				
1 pm	00 15 30 45				
2 pm	00 15 30 45				
3 pm	00 15 30 45				
4 pm	00 15 30 45				
5 pm	00 15 30 45				
6 pm	00 15 30 45				
7 pm	00 15 30 45				
8 pm	00 15 30 45				
9 pm	00 15 30 45				
10 pm	00 15 30 45				

		Fri 23 July	Sat 24 July	Sun 25 July	Notes
6 am	00 15 30 45				
7 am	00 15 30 45				
8 am	00 15 30 45				
9 am	00 15 30 45				
10 am	00 15 30 45				
11 am	00 15 30 45				
12 pm	00 15 30 45				
1 pm	00 15 30 45				
2 pm	00 15 30 45				
3 pm	00 15 30 45				
4 pm	00 15 30 45				
5 pm	00 15 30 45				
6 pm	00 15 30 45				
7 pm	00 15 30 45				
8 pm	00 15 30 45				
9 pm	00 15 30 45				
10 pm	00 15 30 45				

		Mon 26 July	Tue 27 July	Wed 28 July	Thu 29 July
6 am	00 15 30 45				
7 am	00 15 30 45				
8 am	00 15 30 45				
9 am	00 15 30 45				
10 am	00 15 30 45				
11 am	00 15 30 45				
12 pm	00 15 30 45				
1 pm	00 15 30 45				
2 pm	00 15 30 45				
3 pm	00 15 30 45				
4 pm	00 15 30 45				
5 pm	00 15 30 45				
6 pm	00 15 30 45				
7 pm	00 15 30 45				
8 pm	00 15 30 45				
9 pm	00 15 30 45				
10 pm	00 15 30 45				

		Fri	30 July	Sat	31 July	Sun	1 August	Notes
6 am	00 15 30 45							
7 am	00 15 30 45							
8 am	00 15 30 45							
9 am	00 15 30 45							
10 am	00 15 30 45							
11 am	00 15 30 45							
12 pm	00 15 30 45							
1 pm	00 15 30 45							
2 pm	00 15 30 45							
3 pm	00 15 30 45							
4 pm	00 15 30 45							
5 pm	00 15 30 45							
6 pm	00 15 30 45							
7 pm	00 15 30 45							
8 pm	00 15 30 45							
9 pm	00 15 30 45							
10 pm	00 15 30 45							

	Mon 2 August	Tue 3 August	Wed 4 August	Thu 5 August
6 am — 00 15 30 45				
7 am — 00 15 30 45				
8 am — 00 15 30 45				
9 am — 00 15 30 45				
10 am — 00 15 30 45				
11 am — 00 15 30 45				
12 pm — 00 15 30 45				
1 pm — 00 15 30 45				
2 pm — 00 15 30 45				
3 pm — 00 15 30 45				
4 pm — 00 15 30 45				
5 pm — 00 15 30 45				
6 pm — 00 15 30 45				
7 pm — 00 15 30 45				
8 pm — 00 15 30 45				
9 pm — 00 15 30 45				
10 pm — 00 15 30 45				

		Fri 6 August	Sat 7 August	Sun 8 August	Notes
6 am	00 15 30 45				
7 am	00 15 30 45				
8 am	00 15 30 45				
9 am	00 15 30 45				
10 am	00 15 30 45				
11 am	00 15 30 45				
12 pm	00 15 30 45				
1 pm	00 15 30 45				
2 pm	00 15 30 45				
3 pm	00 15 30 45				
4 pm	00 15 30 45				
5 pm	00 15 30 45				
6 pm	00 15 30 45				
7 pm	00 15 30 45				
8 pm	00 15 30 45				
9 pm	00 15 30 45				
10 pm	00 15 30 45				

		Mon 9 August	Tue 10 August	Wed 11 August	Thu 12 August
6 am	00 15 30 45				
7 am	00 15 30 45				
8 am	00 15 30 45				
9 am	00 15 30 45				
10 am	00 15 30 45				
11 am	00 15 30 45				
12 pm	00 15 30 45				
1 pm	00 15 30 45				
2 pm	00 15 30 45				
3 pm	00 15 30 45				
4 pm	00 15 30 45				
5 pm	00 15 30 45				
6 pm	00 15 30 45				
7 pm	00 15 30 45				
8 pm	00 15 30 45				
9 pm	00 15 30 45				
10 pm	00 15 30 45				

	Fri 13 August	Sat 14 August	Sun 15 August	Notes
6 am				
7 am				
8 am				
9 am				
10 am				
11 am				
12 pm				
1 pm				
2 pm				
3 pm				
4 pm				
5 pm				
6 pm				
7 pm				
8 pm				
9 pm				
10 pm				

		Mon 16 August	Tue 17 August	Wed 18 August	Thu 19 August
6 am	00 15 30 45				
7 am	00 15 30 45				
8 am	00 15 30 45				
9 am	00 15 30 45				
10 am	00 15 30 45				
11 am	00 15 30 45				
12 pm	00 15 30 45				
1 pm	00 15 30 45				
2 pm	00 15 30 45				
3 pm	00 15 30 45				
4 pm	00 15 30 45				
5 pm	00 15 30 45				
6 pm	00 15 30 45				
7 pm	00 15 30 45				
8 pm	00 15 30 45				
9 pm	00 15 30 45				
10 pm	00 15 30 45				

	Fri 20 August	Sat 21 August	Sun 22 August	Notes
6 am				
7 am				
8 am				
9 am				
10 am				
11 am				
12 pm				
1 pm				
2 pm				
3 pm				
4 pm				
5 pm				
6 pm				
7 pm				
8 pm				
9 pm				
10 pm				

		Mon 23 August	Tue 24 August	Wed 25 August	Thu 26 August
6 am	00 15 30 45				
7 am	00 15 30 45				
8 am	00 15 30 45				
9 am	00 15 30 45				
10 am	00 15 30 45				
11 am	00 15 30 45				
12 pm	00 15 30 45				
1 pm	00 15 30 45				
2 pm	00 15 30 45				
3 pm	00 15 30 45				
4 pm	00 15 30 45				
5 pm	00 15 30 45				
6 pm	00 15 30 45				
7 pm	00 15 30 45				
8 pm	00 15 30 45				
9 pm	00 15 30 45				
10 pm	00 15 30 45				

		Fri	27 August	Sat	28 August	Sun	29 August	Notes
6 am	00 15 30 45							
7 am	00 15 30 45							
8 am	00 15 30 45							
9 am	00 15 30 45							
10 am	00 15 30 45							
11 am	00 15 30 45							
12 pm	00 15 30 45							
1 pm	00 15 30 45							
2 pm	00 15 30 45							
3 pm	00 15 30 45							
4 pm	00 15 30 45							
5 pm	00 15 30 45							
6 pm	00 15 30 45							
7 pm	00 15 30 45							
8 pm	00 15 30 45							
9 pm	00 15 30 45							
10 pm	00 15 30 45							

	Mon 30 August	Tue 31 August	Wed 1 September	Thu 2 September
6 am				
7 am				
8 am				
9 am				
10 am				
11 am				
12 pm				
1 pm				
2 pm				
3 pm				
4 pm				
5 pm				
6 pm				
7 pm				
8 pm				
9 pm				
10 pm				

		Fri 3 September	Sat 4 September	Sun 5 September	Notes
6 am	00 15 30 45				
7 am	00 15 30 45				
8 am	00 15 30 45				
9 am	00 15 30 45				
10 am	00 15 30 45				
11 am	00 15 30 45				
12 pm	00 15 30 45				
1 pm	00 15 30 45				
2 pm	00 15 30 45				
3 pm	00 15 30 45				
4 pm	00 15 30 45				
5 pm	00 15 30 45				
6 pm	00 15 30 45				
7 pm	00 15 30 45				
8 pm	00 15 30 45				
9 pm	00 15 30 45				
10 pm	00 15 30 45				

		Mon 6 September	Tue 7 September	Wed 8 September	Thu 9 September
6 am	00 15 30 45				
7 am	00 15 30 45				
8 am	00 15 30 45				
9 am	00 15 30 45				
10 am	00 15 30 45				
11 am	00 15 30 45				
12 pm	00 15 30 45				
1 pm	00 15 30 45				
2 pm	00 15 30 45				
3 pm	00 15 30 45				
4 pm	00 15 30 45				
5 pm	00 15 30 45				
6 pm	00 15 30 45				
7 pm	00 15 30 45				
8 pm	00 15 30 45				
9 pm	00 15 30 45				
10 pm	00 15 30 45				

	Fri 10 September	Sat 11 September	Sun 12 September	Notes
6 am				
7 am				
8 am				
9 am				
10 am				
11 am				
12 pm				
1 pm				
2 pm				
3 pm				
4 pm				
5 pm				
6 pm				
7 pm				
8 pm				
9 pm				
10 pm				

	Mon 13 September	Tue 14 September	Wed 15 September	Thu 16 September
6 am				
7 am				
8 am				
9 am				
10 am				
11 am				
12 pm				
1 pm				
2 pm				
3 pm				
4 pm				
5 pm				
6 pm				
7 pm				
8 pm				
9 pm				
10 pm				

	Fri 17 September	Sat 18 September	Sun 19 September	Notes
6 am				
7 am				
8 am				
9 am				
10 am				
11 am				
12 pm				
1 pm				
2 pm				
3 pm				
4 pm				
5 pm				
6 pm				
7 pm				
8 pm				
9 pm				
10 pm				

		Mon 20 September	Tue 21 September	Wed 22 September	Thu 23 September
6 am	00 15 30 45				
7 am	00 15 30 45				
8 am	00 15 30 45				
9 am	00 15 30 45				
10 am	00 15 30 45				
11 am	00 15 30 45				
12 pm	00 15 30 45				
1 pm	00 15 30 45				
2 pm	00 15 30 45				
3 pm	00 15 30 45				
4 pm	00 15 30 45				
5 pm	00 15 30 45				
6 pm	00 15 30 45				
7 pm	00 15 30 45				
8 pm	00 15 30 45				
9 pm	00 15 30 45				
10 pm	00 15 30 45				

	Fri 24 September	Sat 25 September	Sun 26 September	Notes
6 am				
7 am				
8 am				
9 am				
10 am				
11 am				
12 pm				
1 pm				
2 pm				
3 pm				
4 pm				
5 pm				
6 pm				
7 pm				
8 pm				
9 pm				
10 pm				

	Mon 27 September	Tue 28 September	Wed 29 September	Thu 30 September
6 am				
7 am				
8 am				
9 am				
10 am				
11 am				
12 pm				
1 pm				
2 pm				
3 pm				
4 pm				
5 pm				
6 pm				
7 pm				
8 pm				
9 pm				
10 pm				

	Fri 1 October	Sat 2 October	Sun 3 October	Notes
6 am				
7 am				
8 am				
9 am				
10 am				
11 am				
12 pm				
1 pm				
2 pm				
3 pm				
4 pm				
5 pm				
6 pm				
7 pm				
8 pm				
9 pm				
10 pm				

		Mon 4 October	Tue 5 October	Wed 6 October	Thu 7 October
6 am	00 15 30 45				
7 am	00 15 30 45				
8 am	00 15 30 45				
9 am	00 15 30 45				
10 am	00 15 30 45				
11 am	00 15 30 45				
12 pm	00 15 30 45				
1 pm	00 15 30 45				
2 pm	00 15 30 45				
3 pm	00 15 30 45				
4 pm	00 15 30 45				
5 pm	00 15 30 45				
6 pm	00 15 30 45				
7 pm	00 15 30 45				
8 pm	00 15 30 45				
9 pm	00 15 30 45				
10 pm	00 15 30 45				

		Fri	8 October	Sat	9 October	Sun	10 October	Notes
6 am	00 15 30 45							
7 am	00 15 30 45							
8 am	00 15 30 45							
9 am	00 15 30 45							
10 am	00 15 30 45							
11 am	00 15 30 45							
12 pm	00 15 30 45							
1 pm	00 15 30 45							
2 pm	00 15 30 45							
3 pm	00 15 30 45							
4 pm	00 15 30 45							
5 pm	00 15 30 45							
6 pm	00 15 30 45							
7 pm	00 15 30 45							
8 pm	00 15 30 45							
9 pm	00 15 30 45							
10 pm	00 15 30 45							

		Mon 11 October	Tue 12 October	Wed 13 October	Thu 14 October
6 am	00 15 30 45				
7 am	00 15 30 45				
8 am	00 15 30 45				
9 am	00 15 30 45				
10 am	00 15 30 45				
11 am	00 15 30 45				
12 pm	00 15 30 45				
1 pm	00 15 30 45				
2 pm	00 15 30 45				
3 pm	00 15 30 45				
4 pm	00 15 30 45				
5 pm	00 15 30 45				
6 pm	00 15 30 45				
7 pm	00 15 30 45				
8 pm	00 15 30 45				
9 pm	00 15 30 45				
10 pm	00 15 30 45				

	Fri 15 October	Sat 16 October	Sun 17 October	Notes
6 am				
7 am				
8 am				
9 am				
10 am				
11 am				
12 pm				
1 pm				
2 pm				
3 pm				
4 pm				
5 pm				
6 pm				
7 pm				
8 pm				
9 pm				
10 pm				

		Mon 18 October	Tue 19 October	Wed 20 October	Thu 21 October
6 am	00 15 30 45				
7 am	00 15 30 45				
8 am	00 15 30 45				
9 am	00 15 30 45				
10 am	00 15 30 45				
11 am	00 15 30 45				
12 pm	00 15 30 45				
1 pm	00 15 30 45				
2 pm	00 15 30 45				
3 pm	00 15 30 45				
4 pm	00 15 30 45				
5 pm	00 15 30 45				
6 pm	00 15 30 45				
7 pm	00 15 30 45				
8 pm	00 15 30 45				
9 pm	00 15 30 45				
10 pm	00 15 30 45				

		Fri	22 October	Sat	23 October	Sun	24 October	Notes
6 am	00 15 30 45							
7 am	00 15 30 45							
8 am	00 15 30 45							
9 am	00 15 30 45							
10 am	00 15 30 45							
11 am	00 15 30 45							
12 pm	00 15 30 45							
1 pm	00 15 30 45							
2 pm	00 15 30 45							
3 pm	00 15 30 45							
4 pm	00 15 30 45							
5 pm	00 15 30 45							
6 pm	00 15 30 45							
7 pm	00 15 30 45							
8 pm	00 15 30 45							
9 pm	00 15 30 45							
10 pm	00 15 30 45							

	Mon 25 October	Tue 26 October	Wed 27 October	Thu 28 October
6 am				
7 am				
8 am				
9 am				
10 am				
11 am				
12 pm				
1 pm				
2 pm				
3 pm				
4 pm				
5 pm				
6 pm				
7 pm				
8 pm				
9 pm				
10 pm				

		Fri 29 October	Sat 30 October	Sun 31 October	Notes
6 am	00 15 30 45				
7 am	00 15 30 45				
8 am	00 15 30 45				
9 am	00 15 30 45				
10 am	00 15 30 45				
11 am	00 15 30 45				
12 pm	00 15 30 45				
1 pm	00 15 30 45				
2 pm	00 15 30 45				
3 pm	00 15 30 45				
4 pm	00 15 30 45				
5 pm	00 15 30 45				
6 pm	00 15 30 45				
7 pm	00 15 30 45				
8 pm	00 15 30 45				
9 pm	00 15 30 45				
10 pm	00 15 30 45				

		Mon 1 November	Tue 2 November	Wed 3 November	Thu 4 November
6 am	00 15 30 45				
7 am	00 15 30 45				
8 am	00 15 30 45				
9 am	00 15 30 45				
10 am	00 15 30 45				
11 am	00 15 30 45				
12 pm	00 15 30 45				
1 pm	00 15 30 45				
2 pm	00 15 30 45				
3 pm	00 15 30 45				
4 pm	00 15 30 45				
5 pm	00 15 30 45				
6 pm	00 15 30 45				
7 pm	00 15 30 45				
8 pm	00 15 30 45				
9 pm	00 15 30 45				
10 pm	00 15 30 45				

		Fri 5 November	Sat 6 November	Sun 7 November	Notes
6 am	00 15 30 45				
7 am	00 15 30 45				
8 am	00 15 30 45				
9 am	00 15 30 45				
10 am	00 15 30 45				
11 am	00 15 30 45				
12 pm	00 15 30 45				
1 pm	00 15 30 45				
2 pm	00 15 30 45				
3 pm	00 15 30 45				
4 pm	00 15 30 45				
5 pm	00 15 30 45				
6 pm	00 15 30 45				
7 pm	00 15 30 45				
8 pm	00 15 30 45				
9 pm	00 15 30 45				
10 pm	00 15 30 45				

	Mon 8 November	Tue 9 November	Wed 10 November	Thu 11 November
6 am 00 15 30 45				
7 am 00 15 30 45				
8 am 00 15 30 45				
9 am 00 15 30 45				
10 am 00 15 30 45				
11 am 00 15 30 45				
12 pm 00 15 30 45				
1 pm 00 15 30 45				
2 pm 00 15 30 45				
3 pm 00 15 30 45				
4 pm 00 15 30 45				
5 pm 00 15 30 45				
6 pm 00 15 30 45				
7 pm 00 15 30 45				
8 pm 00 15 30 45				
9 pm 00 15 30 45				
10 pm 00 15 30 45				

	Fri 12 November	Sat 13 November	Sun 14 November	Notes
6 am				
7 am				
8 am				
9 am				
10 am				
11 am				
12 pm				
1 pm				
2 pm				
3 pm				
4 pm				
5 pm				
6 pm				
7 pm				
8 pm				
9 pm				
10 pm				

		Mon 15 November	Tue 16 November	Wed 17 November	Thu 18 November
6 am	00 15 30 45				
7 am	00 15 30 45				
8 am	00 15 30 45				
9 am	00 15 30 45				
10 am	00 15 30 45				
11 am	00 15 30 45				
12 pm	00 15 30 45				
1 pm	00 15 30 45				
2 pm	00 15 30 45				
3 pm	00 15 30 45				
4 pm	00 15 30 45				
5 pm	00 15 30 45				
6 pm	00 15 30 45				
7 pm	00 15 30 45				
8 pm	00 15 30 45				
9 pm	00 15 30 45				
10 pm	00 15 30 45				

	Fri 19 November	Sat 20 November	Sun 21 November	Notes
6 am	00 / 15 / 30 / 45			
7 am	00 / 15 / 30 / 45			
8 am	00 / 15 / 30 / 45			
9 am	00 / 15 / 30 / 45			
10 am	00 / 15 / 30 / 45			
11 am	00 / 15 / 30 / 45			
12 pm	00 / 15 / 30 / 45			
1 pm	00 / 15 / 30 / 45			
2 pm	00 / 15 / 30 / 45			
3 pm	00 / 15 / 30 / 45			
4 pm	00 / 15 / 30 / 45			
5 pm	00 / 15 / 30 / 45			
6 pm	00 / 15 / 30 / 45			
7 pm	00 / 15 / 30 / 45			
8 pm	00 / 15 / 30 / 45			
9 pm	00 / 15 / 30 / 45			
10 pm	00 / 15 / 30 / 45			

	Mon 22 November	Tue 23 November	Wed 24 November	Thu 25 November
6 am				
7 am				
8 am				
9 am				
10 am				
11 am				
12 pm				
1 pm				
2 pm				
3 pm				
4 pm				
5 pm				
6 pm				
7 pm				
8 pm				
9 pm				
10 pm				

	Fri 26 November	Sat 27 November	Sun 28 November	Notes
6 am				
7 am				
8 am				
9 am				
10 am				
11 am				
12 pm				
1 pm				
2 pm				
3 pm				
4 pm				
5 pm				
6 pm				
7 pm				
8 pm				
9 pm				
10 pm				

	Mon 29 November	Tue 30 November	Wed 1 December	Thu 2 December
6 am 00 15 30 45				
7 am 00 15 30 45				
8 am 00 15 30 45				
9 am 00 15 30 45				
10 am 00 15 30 45				
11 am 00 15 30 45				
12 pm 00 15 30 45				
1 pm 00 15 30 45				
2 pm 00 15 30 45				
3 pm 00 15 30 45				
4 pm 00 15 30 45				
5 pm 00 15 30 45				
6 pm 00 15 30 45				
7 pm 00 15 30 45				
8 pm 00 15 30 45				
9 pm 00 15 30 45				
10 pm 00 15 30 45				

		Fri	3 December	Sat	4 December	Sun	5 December	Notes
6 am	00 15 30 45							
7 am	00 15 30 45							
8 am	00 15 30 45							
9 am	00 15 30 45							
10 am	00 15 30 45							
11 am	00 15 30 45							
12 pm	00 15 30 45							
1 pm	00 15 30 45							
2 pm	00 15 30 45							
3 pm	00 15 30 45							
4 pm	00 15 30 45							
5 pm	00 15 30 45							
6 pm	00 15 30 45							
7 pm	00 15 30 45							
8 pm	00 15 30 45							
9 pm	00 15 30 45							
10 pm	00 15 30 45							

	Mon 6 December	Tue 7 December	Wed 8 December	Thu 9 December
6 am				
7 am				
8 am				
9 am				
10 am				
11 am				
12 pm				
1 pm				
2 pm				
3 pm				
4 pm				
5 pm				
6 pm				
7 pm				
8 pm				
9 pm				
10 pm				

	Fri 10 December	Sat 11 December	Sun 12 December	Notes
6 am				
7 am				
8 am				
9 am				
10 am				
11 am				
12 pm				
1 pm				
2 pm				
3 pm				
4 pm				
5 pm				
6 pm				
7 pm				
8 pm				
9 pm				
10 pm				

	Mon 13 December	Tue 14 December	Wed 15 December	Thu 16 December
6 am				
7 am				
8 am				
9 am				
10 am				
11 am				
12 pm				
1 pm				
2 pm				
3 pm				
4 pm				
5 pm				
6 pm				
7 pm				
8 pm				
9 pm				
10 pm				

	Fri 17 December	Sat 18 December	Sun 19 December	Notes
6 am				
7 am				
8 am				
9 am				
10 am				
11 am				
12 pm				
1 pm				
2 pm				
3 pm				
4 pm				
5 pm				
6 pm				
7 pm				
8 pm				
9 pm				
10 pm				

		Mon 20 December	Tue 21 December	Wed 22 December	Thu 23 December
6 am	00 15 30 45				
7 am	00 15 30 45				
8 am	00 15 30 45				
9 am	00 15 30 45				
10 am	00 15 30 45				
11 am	00 15 30 45				
12 pm	00 15 30 45				
1 pm	00 15 30 45				
2 pm	00 15 30 45				
3 pm	00 15 30 45				
4 pm	00 15 30 45				
5 pm	00 15 30 45				
6 pm	00 15 30 45				
7 pm	00 15 30 45				
8 pm	00 15 30 45				
9 pm	00 15 30 45				
10 pm	00 15 30 45				

	Fri 24 December	Sat 25 December	Sun 26 December	Notes
6 am 00 / 15 / 30 / 45				
7 am 00 / 15 / 30 / 45				
8 am 00 / 15 / 30 / 45				
9 am 00 / 15 / 30 / 45				
10 am 00 / 15 / 30 / 45				
11 am 00 / 15 / 30 / 45				
12 pm 00 / 15 / 30 / 45				
1 pm 00 / 15 / 30 / 45				
2 pm 00 / 15 / 30 / 45				
3 pm 00 / 15 / 30 / 45				
4 pm 00 / 15 / 30 / 45				
5 pm 00 / 15 / 30 / 45				
6 pm 00 / 15 / 30 / 45				
7 pm 00 / 15 / 30 / 45				
8 pm 00 / 15 / 30 / 45				
9 pm 00 / 15 / 30 / 45				
10 pm 00 / 15 / 30 / 45				

		Mon 27 December	Tue 28 December	Wed 29 December	Thu 30 December
6 am	00 15 30 45				
7 am	00 15 30 45				
8 am	00 15 30 45				
9 am	00 15 30 45				
10 am	00 15 30 45				
11 am	00 15 30 45				
12 pm	00 15 30 45				
1 pm	00 15 30 45				
2 pm	00 15 30 45				
3 pm	00 15 30 45				
4 pm	00 15 30 45				
5 pm	00 15 30 45				
6 pm	00 15 30 45				
7 pm	00 15 30 45				
8 pm	00 15 30 45				
9 pm	00 15 30 45				
10 pm	00 15 30 45				

		Fri 31 December	Sat 1 January	Sun 2 January	Notes
6 am	00 15 30 45				
7 am	00 15 30 45				
8 am	00 15 30 45				
9 am	00 15 30 45				
10 am	00 15 30 45				
11 am	00 15 30 45				
12 pm	00 15 30 45				
1 pm	00 15 30 45				
2 pm	00 15 30 45				
3 pm	00 15 30 45				
4 pm	00 15 30 45				
5 pm	00 15 30 45				
6 pm	00 15 30 45				
7 pm	00 15 30 45				
8 pm	00 15 30 45				
9 pm	00 15 30 45				
10 pm	00 15 30 45				

Contacts LIST

NAME:
PHONE:
ADDRESS:

EMAIL:

NAME:
PHONE:
ADDRESS:

EMAIL:

NAME:
PHONE:
ADDRESS:

EMAIL:

NAME:
PHONE:
ADDRESS:

EMAIL:

NAME:
PHONE:
ADDRESS:

EMAIL:

NAME:
PHONE:
ADDRESS:

EMAIL:

NAME:
PHONE:
ADDRESS:

EMAIL:

NAME:
PHONE:
ADDRESS:

EMAIL:

NAME:
PHONE:
ADDRESS:

EMAIL:

NAME:
PHONE:
ADDRESS:

EMAIL:

NAME:
PHONE:
ADDRESS:

EMAIL:

NAME:
PHONE:
ADDRESS:

EMAIL:

NAME:
PHONE:
ADDRESS:

EMAIL:

NAME:
PHONE:
ADDRESS:

EMAIL:

Contacts LIST

NAME:
PHONE:
ADDRESS:

EMAIL:

NAME:
PHONE:
ADDRESS:

EMAIL:

NAME:
PHONE:
ADDRESS:

EMAIL:

NAME:
PHONE:
ADDRESS:

EMAIL:

NAME:
PHONE:
ADDRESS:

EMAIL:

NAME:
PHONE:
ADDRESS:

EMAIL:

NAME:
PHONE:
ADDRESS:

EMAIL:

NAME:
PHONE:
ADDRESS:

EMAIL:

NAME:
PHONE:
ADDRESS:

EMAIL:

NAME:
PHONE:
ADDRESS:

EMAIL:

NAME:
PHONE:
ADDRESS:

EMAIL:

NAME:
PHONE:
ADDRESS:

EMAIL:

NAME:
PHONE:
ADDRESS:

EMAIL:

NAME:
PHONE:
ADDRESS:

EMAIL:

Contacts LIST

NAME:
PHONE:
ADDRESS:

EMAIL:

NAME:
PHONE:
ADDRESS:

EMAIL:

NAME:
PHONE:
ADDRESS:

EMAIL:

NAME:
PHONE:
ADDRESS:

EMAIL:

NAME:
PHONE:
ADDRESS:

EMAIL:

NAME:
PHONE:
ADDRESS:

EMAIL:

NAME:
PHONE:
ADDRESS:

EMAIL:

NAME:
PHONE:
ADDRESS:

EMAIL:

NAME:
PHONE:
ADDRESS:

EMAIL:

NAME:
PHONE:
ADDRESS:

EMAIL:

NAME:
PHONE:
ADDRESS:

EMAIL:

NAME:
PHONE:
ADDRESS:

EMAIL:

NAME:
PHONE:
ADDRESS:

EMAIL:

NAME:
PHONE:
ADDRESS:

EMAIL:

Contacts LIST

NAME:		NAME:	
PHONE:		PHONE:	
ADDRESS:		ADDRESS:	
EMAIL:		EMAIL:	

NAME:		NAME:	
PHONE:		PHONE:	
ADDRESS:		ADDRESS:	
EMAIL:		EMAIL:	

NAME:		NAME:	
PHONE:		PHONE:	
ADDRESS:		ADDRESS:	
EMAIL:		EMAIL:	

NAME:		NAME:	
PHONE:		PHONE:	
ADDRESS:		ADDRESS:	
EMAIL:		EMAIL:	

NAME:		NAME:	
PHONE:		PHONE:	
ADDRESS:		ADDRESS:	
EMAIL:		EMAIL:	

NAME:		NAME:	
PHONE:		PHONE:	
ADDRESS:		ADDRESS:	
EMAIL:		EMAIL:	

NAME:		NAME:	
PHONE:		PHONE:	
ADDRESS:		ADDRESS:	
EMAIL:		EMAIL:	

Contacts LIST

NAME:		NAME:	
PHONE:		PHONE:	
ADDRESS:		ADDRESS:	
EMAIL:		EMAIL:	

NAME:		NAME:	
PHONE:		PHONE:	
ADDRESS:		ADDRESS:	
EMAIL:		EMAIL:	

NAME:		NAME:	
PHONE:		PHONE:	
ADDRESS:		ADDRESS:	
EMAIL:		EMAIL:	

NAME:		NAME:	
PHONE:		PHONE:	
ADDRESS:		ADDRESS:	
EMAIL:		EMAIL:	

NAME:		NAME:	
PHONE:		PHONE:	
ADDRESS:		ADDRESS:	
EMAIL:		EMAIL:	

NAME:		NAME:	
PHONE:		PHONE:	
ADDRESS:		ADDRESS:	
EMAIL:		EMAIL:	

NAME:		NAME:	
PHONE:		PHONE:	
ADDRESS:		ADDRESS:	
EMAIL:		EMAIL:	

Passwords

Website	
Username	
Password	
Email	
Notes	

Website	
Username	
Password	
Email	
Notes	

Website	
Username	
Password	
Email	
Notes	

Website	
Username	
Password	
Email	
Notes	

Website	
Username	
Password	
Email	
Notes	

Website	
Username	
Password	
Email	
Notes	

Website	
Username	
Password	
Email	
Notes	

Website	
Username	
Password	
Email	
Notes	

Passwords

Website	
Username	
Password	
Email	
Notes	

Website	
Username	
Password	
Email	
Notes	

Website	
Username	
Password	
Email	
Notes	

Website	
Username	
Password	
Email	
Notes	

Website	
Username	
Password	
Email	
Notes	

Website	
Username	
Password	
Email	
Notes	

Website	
Username	
Password	
Email	
Notes	

Website	
Username	
Password	
Email	
Notes	

Passwords

Website

Username	
Password	
Email	
Notes	

Website

Username	
Password	
Email	
Notes	

Website

Username	
Password	
Email	
Notes	

Website

Username	
Password	
Email	
Notes	

Website

Username	
Password	
Email	
Notes	

Website

Username	
Password	
Email	
Notes	

Website

Username	
Password	
Email	
Notes	

Website

Username	
Password	
Email	
Notes	

Passwords

Website

Username	
Password	
Email	
Notes	

Website

Username	
Password	
Email	
Notes	

Website

Username	
Password	
Email	
Notes	

Website

Username	
Password	
Email	
Notes	

Website

Username	
Password	
Email	
Notes	

Website

Username	
Password	
Email	
Notes	

Website

Username	
Password	
Email	
Notes	

Website

Username	
Password	
Email	
Notes	

Passwords

Website

Username

Password

Email

Notes

Website

Username

Password

Email

Notes

Website

Username

Password

Email

Notes

Website

Username

Password

Email

Notes

Website

Username

Password

Email

Notes

Website

Username

Password

Email

Notes

Website

Username

Password

Email

Notes

Website

Username

Password

Email

Notes

Made in the USA
Monee, IL
25 June 2021